Count Me In!

What's for Lunch?

Lisa Greathouse

Consultant

Timothy Rasinski, Ph.D.
Kent State University

Publishing Credits

Dona Herweck Rice, *Editor-in-Chief*

Robin Erickson, *Production Director*

Lee Aucoin, *Creative Director*

Conni Medina, M.A.Ed., *Editorial Director*

Jamey Acosta, *Editor*

Stephanie Reid, *Photo Editor*

Rachelle Cracchiolo, M.S.Ed., *Publisher*

Based on writing from *TIME For Kids*.

TIME For Kids and the *TIME For Kids* logo are registered trademarks of TIME Inc. Used under license.

Teacher Created Materials

5301 Oceanus Drive
Huntington Beach, CA 92649-1030
http://www.tcmpub.com

ISBN 978-1-4333-3639-3

© 2012 Teacher Created Materials, Inc.

Table of Contents

Is It Time for Lunch Yet?

Is that your stomach growling? It's been hours since you ate breakfast. You are getting hungrier by the minute. You look at the clock on the classroom wall. It's almost time for lunch!

Time to Eat

Time to Play

Time to Go
Back to Class

Make Every Minute Count

If you have a total of 45 minutes to eat lunch and play, and it takes you 20 minutes to eat, how much time is left to play?

45 – 20 = 25 minutes

Lunchbox or Lunch Line?

Will you have pizza or a peanut butter and jelly sandwich? A burrito (buh-REE-toh) or ham and cheese?

Some kids bring lunch from home. Some get their lunch in the school **cafeteria** (kaf-i-TEER-ee-uh).

Any Way You Cut It!

Do you like your sandwich cut into halves or quarters? Do you like it cut diagonally into triangles? What other shapes could you make from your sandwich?

1 whole

one-half $\frac{1}{2}$

one-half
cut diagonally

one-fourth $\frac{1}{4}$

cut into a heart

Monday	Tuesday	Wednesda
pasta with sauce tossed salad apple crisp	tomato soup breadsticks peaches	turkey sandwich pasta salad fresh fruit bowl
grilled cheese corn chilled peaches	Italian sub carrot sticks grapes	cheese pizza Caesar salad apples
cheese pizza Caesar salad apples	turkey wrap baby carrots fresh fruit bowl	bean burrito rice applesauce
tuna sandwich carrot sticks fruit salad	chicken salad breadsticks grapes	spaghetti breadsticks peaches

What's on the Menu?

Does your school lunch menu look something like this? Which meal is offered the greatest number of times?

The good thing about buying lunch at school is that it will be just the right temperature when you get it. The bad thing is that you might not always like what's on the menu. And you can't get seconds!

Thursday	Friday
cheese pizza Caesar salad apples	BBQ chicken baby carrots berries
chicken salad pinto beans apple cobbler	cheese ravioli veggie dippers berries
spaghetti breadsticks peaches	turkey sub pasta salad apples
grilled cheese pasta salad pudding	cheese pizza Caesar salad apples

Sometimes the lunch lines are long. Take a look at the line in the picture above. If it takes each student two minutes to get through the line, how long will it take for the last student in line to get his or her lunch?

4 students x 2 minutes each = 8 minutes

What's Cooking?

Some foods need to be kept hot or cold to keep them safe to eat. Otherwise, harmful **bacteria** (bak-TEER-ee-uh) can grow and make you sick.

Make Sure It's Safe!

To be safe to eat, a hamburger should be cooked to 160°F. The milk you drink with it should be kept below 45°F. A food thermometer measures the temperature of your food.

The cafeteria staff makes sure hot foods stay hot and cold foods stay cold. If you bring your lunch, you can put an ice pack in your lunchbox to keep it cold. You can keep food warm in a thermos.

If you buy lunch at school, this may be one of the items in your family's **budget**.

A budget shows how much money you have and how much you spend on each thing you need. You can make a budget for a week, a month, or even a year.

May

Sun.	Mon.	Tues.	Wed.	Thurs.	Fri.	Sat.
1	2 Buy lunch.	3 Buy lunch.	4	5 Buy lunch.	6 Buy lunch.	7
8	9 Buy lunch.	10 Buy lunch.	11	12 Buy lunch.	13 Buy lunch.	14
15	16	17 Buy lunch.	18 Buy lunch.	19 Buy lunch.	20	21
22	23 Buy lunch.	24 Buy lunch.	25	26 Buy lunch.	27 Buy lunch.	28
29	30 Buy lunch.	31				

Your Lunch Budget

Let's say your school lunch costs $2. If you plan to buy lunch 16 days this month, how much do you need to budget for the month?

$2.00 x 16 days = $32.00

Time to Refuel

It's fun to have lunch with your friends. But lunch is also a time for your body to get the **energy** it needs to get through the rest of the day.

How Has the Lunchbox Changed?

Your lunchbox might have a picture of your favorite TV or movie character. But lunchboxes have been used since the early 1900s. They started as plain metal boxes with a handle.

Just like a car needs gasoline to drive, the food you eat fuels your body. Eating a healthy lunch gives your body the **nutrients** (NOO-tree-uhnts) it needs to perform its best.

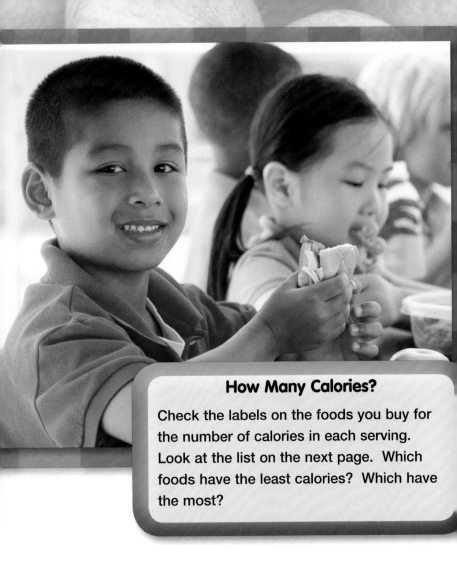

How Many Calories?

Check the labels on the foods you buy for the number of calories in each serving. Look at the list on the next page. Which foods have the least calories? Which have the most?

All foods have **calories**. A calorie measures the energy in what we eat and drink. You need calories to grow. But not all calories are the same!

Food	Calories
apple	45
apple pie (1 slice)	405
banana	100
broccoli (1 cup)	30
burrito	450
carrots (1 cup)	50
ice cream shake	360
cheeseburger	350
cheese pizza (1 slice)	290
chocolate milk	210
cola (12 ounces)	160
French fries (small)	210
potato chips (1 small bag)	130

Foods like fruits, vegetables, beans, and whole grains give your body the **vitamins** and **minerals** it needs. Soda and sweets have lots of calories but none of the nutrients. Too much of any food will make you gain weight, and you won't feel well, either.

My Plate

Knowing what to eat every day to stay healthy can be confusing. The food plate helps us figure it all out. Check out **http://www.choosemyplate.gov** to learn more about healthy food choices.

ChooseMyPlate.gov

If you eat a school lunch, try to look at the menu ahead of time so you can figure out the best choices in advance. If you eat the fruits and vegetables on your tray, you'll be off to a great start!

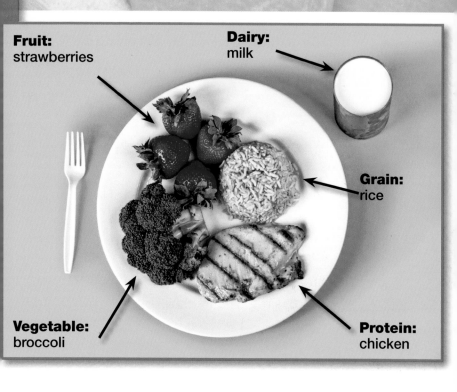

Fruit:
strawberries

Dairy:
milk

Grain:
rice

Vegetable:
broccoli

Protein:
chicken

Here is a meal you might see on your lunch menu. See how each food item fits into the food groups.

This lunch has foods from five of the food groups.

Make It Yourself

Here is an example of a delicious, healthy lunch you can make at home:

- Turkey and vegetables in whole wheat pita bread (250 cal)

- 1 medium orange (60 cal)

- 1 cup fat-free milk (90 cal)

There is a total of 400 calories in this lunch.

250 + 60 + 90 = 400

Most kids your age need about 1,600 calories each day. That means that this lunch is about one-fourth of the total calories needed for the day.

Reading Labels

Almost all foods have a Nutrition Facts label. It tells us what is in the food. It lists calories and fat. But it also lists vitamins, **protein**, and **fiber**. Some numbers are in **percentages**. This tells us what percent of each nutrient we need each day is in that food.

Nutrition Facts

Serving Size 1/4 Cup (30g)
Servings Per Container About 38

Amount Per Serving

Calories 200 Calories from Fat 150

	% Daily Value*
Total Fat 17g	**26%**
Saturated Fat 2.5g	**13%**
Trans Fat 0g	
Cholesterol 0mg	**0%**
Sodium 120mg	**5%**
Total Carbohydrate 7g	**2%**
Dietary Fiber 2g	**8%**
Sugars 1g	
Protein 5g	

Vitamin A 0%	•	Vitamin C 0%
Calcium 4%	•	Iron 8%

*Percent Daily Values are based on a 2,000 calorie diet.

What are you going to drink with your lunch? Your body loses water during the day, so it's important to replace it. But should you drink juice, milk, or water?

Say "No" to Soda

Try to make soda a special treat.   A can of soda has about 10 teaspoons of sugar!

Water is a great choice. Low-fat or fat-free white milk is good for you, too. Flavored milks, fruit drinks, and even some sports drinks have lots of added sugar. If you drink juice, make sure it's 100 percent fruit juice.

Time for Recess!

The only thing at school better than lunch is recess! Not only is it fun, it's also good for you!

Do you like to play dodge ball? How about jumping rope? Playing tag or hopscotch?

Fit for Life

Being fit does more than make you feel good. It keeps your heart healthy and makes your bones and muscles strong.

Whatever you choose to do, the important thing is that you get moving. Try to be active for at least 60 minutes a day. If you play for 20 minutes at recess, that's one-third of your activity for the day.

Be Good to Earth

Make Your School Green!

Many states have recycling programs that will pay you for empty bottles and cans. Some schools have recycling programs to raise money for field trips or to plant trees.

Think about how full the trashcans are after lunch at your school. Wouldn't it be great to cut down on the amount of garbage your school sends to the **landfill**?

One thing you can do is pack your lunch in **reusable** containers. Does your school recycle? If not, ask your teacher if your class can start a recycling program to collect empty water bottles, juice boxes, and more!

Glossary

bacteria—the microscopic organisms that have one cell

budget—a plan for how much money will be earned and spent in a certain period of time

calories—the units for measuring the amount of energy that a food can produce

cafeteria— a lunchroom where people serve themselves or are served at a counter but carry their own food to their tables

energy—the power or ability to make something work or be active

fiber—a mostly indigestible material in food that helps move food through the intestines

landfill—a place used for waste disposal

minerals—non-living elements that are needed to help the body function

nutrients—something in food that helps people, animals, and plants live and grow

percentages—parts of a whole expressed in hundredths

protein—found in chicken, meat, and other foods, protein builds up the tissues in your body

reusable—something that can be used again

vitamins—human-made substances the body needs for good health